An Upside-Down Life

Written by Jo Windsor

Look at this sloth.
A sloth can go upside down.
A sloth has long claws.
The claws help the sloth
to hold on to the tree.

claws

Sloths like to live in trees. They eat the leaves on the trees for their food. Some sloths sleep in the day and wake up at night.

Sloths are very slow.
They are not good at walking on the ground.
But a sloth is good at swimming.

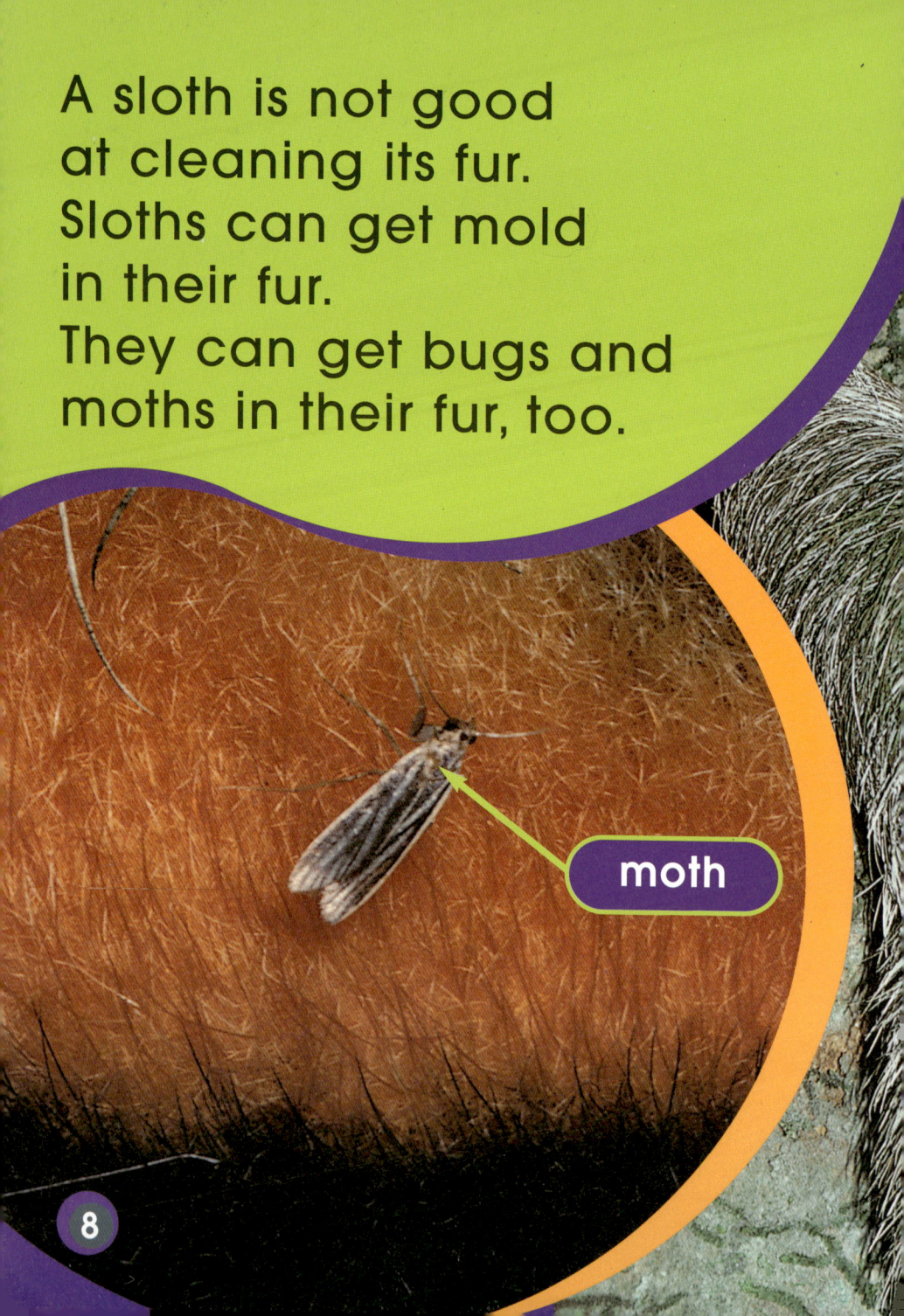

A sloth is not good at cleaning its fur. Sloths can get mold in their fur.
They can get bugs and moths in their fur, too.

moth

A sloth leaves
its droppings
on the ground.
The moths lay eggs
in the droppings.
Little grubs come
out of the eggs.
They will turn into moths.

This is a mother sloth.
She has one baby.
The baby drinks
its mother's milk.
The baby stays
with its mother.

One day the baby will hang upside down. It will not be good at cleaning its fur. It will be like its mother.

Index

baby sloths 12, 14
claws 2
how sloths move 6
what sloths can have
  in their fur
    bugs 8
    moths 8, 10
    mold 8
what sloths eat 4
where sloths
  live 4

Guide Notes

Title: An Upside-Down Life
Stage: Early (3) – Blue

Genre: Nonfiction (Expository)
Approach: Guided Reading
Processes: Thinking Critically, Exploring Language, Processing Information
Written and Visual Focus: Photographs (static images), Labels, Index

THINKING CRITICALLY
(sample questions)
- Look at the front cover and the title. Ask the children: "What do you think this book could be about?"
- Ask the children what they know about sloths.
- Focus the children's attention on the Index. Ask: "What are you going to find out about in this book?"
- If you want to find out about what sloths eat, on which page would you look?
- If you want to find out about what sloths have in their fur, on which pages would you look?
- Look at pages 2 and 3. How do claws help the sloth hold on tight?
- Look at pages 6 and 7. Why do you think sloths are not good at walking on the ground?
- Why do you think mold grows in the sloth's fur?

EXPLORING LANGUAGE

Terminology
Title, cover, photographs, author, photographers

Vocabulary
Interest words: sloth, claws, fur, mold, bugs, moths, droppings, grubs
High-frequency words (new): long, eat, day
Positional words: down, in, on

Print Conventions
Capital letter for sentence beginnings, periods, commas, ellipsis